DRAWING OUT THE DRAGONS

A MEDITATION ON ART, DESTINY, AND THE POWER OF CHOICE

OTHER BOOKS BY JAMES A. OWEN

THE CHRONICLES OF THE IMAGINARIUM GEOGRAPHICA

Book One: Here, There Be Dragons
Book Two: The Search for the Red Dragon
Book Three: The Indigo King
Book Four: The Shadow Dragons
Book Five: The Dragon's Apprentice
Book Six: The Dragons of Winter
Book Seven: The First Dragon (Forthcoming)

Lost Treasures of the Pirates of the Caribbean
(With Jeremy Owen)

*Mapping the Imagination: Annotating the Chronicles of
the Imaginarium Geographica* (Forthcoming)

MYTHWORLD

Book One: The Festival of Bones
Book Two: Invisible Moon
Book Three: Babylon's Meridians
Book Four: The Winter Room

The Unusual Motion of Strange Beasts: Collected Short Stories

The Complete Essential Starchild

Fool's Hollow: Book One (Forthcoming)

DRAWING OUT THE DRAGONS

A MEDITATION ON ART, DESTINY, AND THE POWER OF CHOICE

JAMES A. OWEN

SHADOW
MOUNTAIN

The original edition of this title was published by Coppervale International, LLC, in 2011. Original electronic edition was published in March 2011.

© 2013 Coppervale International, LLC

Visit us at ShadowMountain.com

Library of Congress Cataloging-in-Publication Data

(CIP on file)
ISBN 978-1-60907-368-8

Printed in the United States of America
R. R. Donnelley, Crawfordsville, IN

10   9   8   7   6   5   4   3   2   1

To Elliot S! Maggin,
who knows why I wear a Superman ring

ACKNOWLEDGMENTS

The author wishes to thank Nat Gertler, Daanon DeCock, Angela Hunt, Jason Warren, Jeremy Owen, Victoria Morris, Heidi Berthiaume, and whoever it was that invented caffeine for their help in preparing the original version of this book. Thanks also to my publisher, Chris Schoebinger; my editor, Lisa Mangum; my designer, Richard Erickson, and his team (Hannah Burr, Sheryl Dickert Smith, and Kayla Hackett); and my typographers, Rachael Ward and Malina Grigg, for making this beautiful new edition happen. Thanks to Chuck and Beate Chapman for letting me wreck their car, and to Cindy Owen for earning a grateful acknowledgment more than anyone else could.

INTRODUCTION

I am often asked to speak at schools, and I find that the teachers, librarians, and booksellers who invite me to speak are often surprised that I very rarely speak about my novels. At *all*. There's a good reason for that. The reason is because I believe that there are reading groups, dedicated librarians, community-active booksellers, and, best of all, excellent teachers who are all more than happy to discuss the Dragons, and myths, and legends, and storytelling in my books with their students. So if I am given the attention of five hundred middle-school students for an hour, and only that hour, I'm not going to talk about my novels. I'm going to talk about the things that I believe are most important, the things which have served me well in the course I have taken in this life.

I'm going to talk about the things I believe are most true, and meaningful, and worth sharing. I'm going to tell them stories drawn from my own life: examples about overcoming obstacles and adversity, stories about how making choices in life is like drawing a Dragon, and vignettes about heritage and destiny, and ultimately how I came to do what it is that I love most in the world for my job.

That's an incredibly important point. It's part of what makes giving a motivational talk geared towards middle-school-aged listeners (and older) so significant to me: I love to make illustrations. I love to tell stories. And I believe there's nothing better in the world than getting to do what you love the most for your job.

The choices I've made in my life and career are what allow me to do that, and those choices are a large part of the stories I want to share. I want the people who hear me speak and read what I write to understand that our lives are nothing *but* a series of *choices*—and that you always, *always,* have the chance to choose a different path.

Stories are how we communicate to others the choices we have made; they are part of what bind us together as communities, as cultures, and as the never-ending family we call the Human Race. To me, stories are also the best way to convey what I believe is most necessary for one human being to communicate to another, and I think it's the most significant thing that I can say to anyone: *I believe in you. And I will not let you fall.*

Sometimes, being told that, by someone we trust, is what we need most in our lives. And sometimes just believing that, even for an instant, may mean the difference between a terrible choice and a redemptive one, especially for someone who is so beaten down by despair and hopelessness that they don't realize how many choices they still have. How many choices they have *always* had.

Until now, most readers could not hear that message unless they attended a school, or some signing event where I was speaking, which is why I have long considered putting these stories, these things I most believe, into a book.

A book that is, I feel, the most meaningful thing I've ever written.

I have always believed that if you create and offer something of value, people will return that value to you tenfold, a hundredfold, and more. Those who have heard my presentations, or who have been inspired by my writings, either online or in my books, know—*know*—that Magic is *real* . . . and worth looking for. It exists in the world, and there are people who know how to show you where it is.

I hope that with this book, I might be one of those

people for you. I'd like to show each and every one of you that you can make the same kinds of choices that I did. Our paths may be different, and everyone's mileage varies, but none of us is in competition with anyone else. All we are here to do is find our purpose and make the choices that keep us on as straight a path towards fulfilling that purpose as we can.

Share the Magic that you find in this book. And, hopefully, it will inspire you to make more good choices in your own life and help you see that the Magic isn't hard to find, after all. Because it's *everywhere*. And sometimes, in order to see it, you just need someone you believe in, someone you trust, to take you by the hand, look into your eyes, and say, "I believe in you. And I will not let you fall."

At the very least, I hope you'll enjoy some entertaining stories, and possibly learn how to draw a Dragon. But it's also possible that there's a story in this book that you need to hear, right now. That alone is reason enough not to wait to share these—the most valuable stories I have—because all it takes is a moment of belief, a moment of true Magic, to make the difference.

In a moment, with a single brave choice, your world can *change*—and you, too, can begin to lead an extraordinary life.

PROLOGUE

The real tragedy was
that I'd finally figured out
how to program all the good
stations on the radio.

I barely remember the accident at all.

It unwinds in my memory in slow motion: driving down the street, adjusting the radio, noticing that suddenly a car was turning where it shouldn't be. Then, the impact. I remember being immediately worried about the girl who had made the illegal left-hand turn in front of me, and who was standing outside my window in hysterics, asking if I was all right. My door was stuck, but I was more irritated that something had smashed the radio, as I'd finally just figured out how to program all the good stations.

I remember being embarrassed that the car was blocking traffic, and trying to push it out of the intersection before one of the drivers from the opposite lane who had stopped to help convinced me that I should leave it as is, sit down on the curb, and wait for the ambulance that could be heard in the distance. It was only then that I noticed the numbness that ran along the length of my right arm.

The trip to the hospital was a blur, my memories hazy with dread about how I was going to explain to my friend Chuck that I'd just wrecked his car. I never noticed the brace that was on my right arm until the doctor began speaking to me.

Apparently, when my car smashed into the young lady's car, my hand had smashed into the radio, which wrecked both the radio and my hand.

My drawing hand.

The doctor came into the room with a clipboard in his hand and a cheerful expression on his face.

"You're pretty lucky," he said, looking over the notes on his clipboard. "That was a pretty nasty accident, but the other driver wasn't hurt at all, and it seems all you've broken is your right hand. Like I said," he repeated, "lucky."

"How bad is it?" I asked, not quite daring to look directly at my arm.

"There's been a lot of damage," he replied matter-of-factly, gesturing at an X-ray. "The bones in the joints of your first two fingers were crushed. We could do surgery, but that would create scar tissue and complicate your rehabilitation. The good news is that we were able to set the bones, and, once they heal and you complete a year or so of therapy, you ought to have at least thirty or forty percent of the use back."

"Ah," I replied. "That doesn't sound so good."

The doctor frowned, irritated that I wasn't happier with his prognosis. "It's very good," he said as he headed for the door. "Unless, you know, you rely on your right hand being at a hundred percent to do your job."

"Actually," I said pointedly, "I do. I'm a comic book artist."

The doctor stopped in the doorway and glanced back at me. "No," he said, shaking his head. "Not anymore you're not."

But yield who will to their separation,
My object in living is to unite
My avocation and my vocation
As my two eyes make one in sight.

ROBERT FROST

*Keep away from those who
try to belittle your ambitions.
Small people always do that,
but the really great make you believe
that you too can become great.*

MARK TWAIN

PART I

If you really want to do
something, no one
can stop you.

But if you really don't want
to do something, no one
can help you.

What you can do,
or dream you can do,
begin it;

Boldness has genius,
power, and magic
in it.

GOETHE

CHAPTER ONE

ALL YOUR CHOICES ARE CUMULATIVE

One of the reasons I like talking to middle school students the most is because I actually started my career when I was their age. I started working professionally when I was very, very young. I think it's important to communicate to young people that anything you want to do with your life, whatever you want to achieve, can be started right now.

I started this, started this entire path, this entire career that has led me to writing *Here, There Be Dragons* and the sequels in the Chronicles of the Imaginarium Geographica series, when I was their age.

At age sixteen, I was the youngest professional publisher ever to be an exhibitor at the San Diego Comic-Con. This whole idea of starting things young isn't something I read about in a book, or something I heard about from someone else, it's something that I actually *did*.

And I was able to do it because of the choices I made.

Everything we do in our lives has to do with the choices we've made, and those choices are cumulative. Every choice you make builds a foundation for every choice that follows. And the earlier you realize that you are *always* able to make choices, the earlier you'll be able to build that foundation for everything you want to do with your life. That's important because in our lives, not everyone realizes that *everything* they do is a choice—that you get to *choose* the direction things go.

Yes, our lives don't always go the way we want them to. Bad things happen, obstacles arise, problems spring up to confound our well-laid plans. But how you deal with them is *always* in your power to do. It's always in your power to choose your destiny. To choose how you respond.

I'm both the writer *and* the illustrator of the Chronicles of the Imaginarium Geographica series. That's a very unusual thing. Not many authors are allowed to even have a say in the look of their books, much less have a free hand in illustrating them. They might have a voice in the cover, but for an author to illustrate their own book is unusual. One of the reasons I'm able to do that is because of the experience I gained from writing and illustrating the *StarChild* comic book series. But really, the roots of that ability actually go a bit deeper.

I grew up in a family of artists. My mother was a first-grade teacher who painted. We had an easel with oil paints in the kitchen when I was growing up, and the house always smelled like turpentine. Her older brother was a painter; he painted Native American Kachina dancers. Her other brother was a printer, and her sister was a graphic designer. It was my aunt who became my first artistic mentor, and I apprenticed to her as an artist at the age of thirteen. I basically learned everything I needed to know about illustrating and painting from family gatherings at my grandparents' house.

Our artistic traits came with a pedigree. Our family, the Milletts, claimed both a direct ancestor—the famed turn-of-the-century designer, painter, and journalist, Francis Davis Millet—and a distant cousin—the famed French post-impressionist Jean Francois Millet—as the cornerstones of our artistic heritage.

We apparently had a rebellious side as well, with two American ancestors adding a "t" to the last name to avoid the French pronunciation: Artemus Millett, who converted to the Mormon faith at the behest of Brigham

Young and helped construct the church's temple in Kirtland, Ohio; and John Millett, a knight who, early in the seventeenth century, was awarded the family motto "This hand is hostile to tyrants," and a family crest that depicted an armored hand . . .

. . . grasping the throat of a *Dragon*.

If you add in the other family line that's descended from Cotton Mather, who, in addition to authoring more than 400 books in his lifetime, was also one of the principal antagonists involved in the Salem Witch Trials, then it seems almost a foregone conclusion that I'd end up starting a career in comic books.

In addition to a history of art and rebellion, I also apparently had inherited a strong entrepreneurial streak, and when I was fairly young at that. I started my first publishing venture when I was only six years old. That's absolutely true.

I wrote and illustrated a version of *Goldilocks and the Three Bears,* as well as *Little Red Riding Hood* (both of which, inexplicably, involved Santa Claus, in what was perhaps my first attempt at mixing mythologies). I put the books in a little red wagon and wheeled them around to the neighbors up and down the block, and I sold the books for fifteen cents apiece.

A couple of years ago, a friend of mine was cleaning out his mother's attic and came across one of the *Goldilocks* books. He put it up for auction online, which was where I found it.

It was correctly listed as James Owen's first published work—which I thought was wicked cool—so I put a bid on it, and immediately got a message that I'd been outbid.

So, I put in another bid. And somebody else outbid me *again*. It got down to the last few minutes of the auction, and besides myself there were *four other people* frantically bidding on this little booklet drawn by a six-year-old kid.

And finally, the book sold for $72—and I *lost* it. I sent a message to the fellow who'd bought it and asked if he realized I was the one he'd been bidding against. He said no, he hadn't known that. I told him that I'd *really* love to have that little book if he'd be willing to sell it. He said he'd love to sell it to me, except that now he had a pretty complete James Owen collection; he asked if it would be okay if he just sent me a scan of it.

I said yes, that was totally okay because it was something he'd really wanted, and I thought he should have it.

That was the first book I actually remember doing for money. And to a creative person, money is important. Don't get me wrong—it's *great* to be an artist. It's great to do something creative and put beautiful things out into the world. But if you want to make a living as an artist, you have to think about it as a business as well. You have to make choices that will let you think of it as a career and not just an artistic venture. That is why the *Goldilocks* story is significant: because that little booklet was not in any way, shape, or form worth ten dollars, let alone more than seventy. (Except maybe to my mom, but she already has one.) It was clever, sure (it had Santa Claus in it), but it was still a storybook written and drawn by a first-grader. And yet, it was worth in excess of *fifty* bucks to at least four different collectors.

But not because of what it was.

The value of *Goldilocks* was applied retroactively because of all the creative work I have done in the years since then. The work I've done as an adult has made the work I've done as a teenager, and even as a weird little kid, more valuable.

The choices I made later in life made my earlier choices more worthwhile. Choices are cumulative—and the sooner you realize that, the sooner you are able to start actively making choices that may not only improve your future, but can, in some ways, even redeem mistakes made in the past.

Sometimes people feel their choices are forced upon them. Sometimes circumstances are out of your control, but you can always choose how you respond to them.

There are several key messages I'm hoping to impart to you with this book, messages that I hope you'll take to heart and remember. One of the key messages I want to share, something that I absolutely believe with all my heart, is this: If you really, really want to do something, no one can stop you. But if you really don't want to do something, then no one can help you. The choice is always entirely up to you.

The way I learned that particular lesson was by confronting a few obstacles early in my life. Those obstacles—and how I chose to face them—helped shape all the choices I made later.

We remember our dead.
When they were born,
when they passed away—either
as men of promise,
or as men of achievement.

DAG HAMMARSKJOLD

CHAPTER TWO

PAIN IS ONLY WEAKNESS LEAVING YOUR BODY

When I was about eleven years old, I had some circumstances forced upon me that seemed to limit a great many choices. I came down with a rare blood cell disorder that made me very, very ill. Among other things, it gave me migraine headaches and made me allergic to *everything*. I had to carry around a syringe and epinephrine, and I learned how to give myself injections by basically poking the needle into oranges until I got the hang of it. This was necessary because if I had an allergy attack, I usually had about ninety seconds before my throat would swell closed.

That was usually triggered by a food allergy, but pretty much everything else made me just as sick. I was allergic to perfume, flowers, cigarette smoke, my dog, pizza. (That was the real tragedy, being allergic to pizza.) I was allergic enough, and got sick enough, that I ended up spending a good part of my fifth grade school year in Good Samaritan Hospital in Phoenix. The doctors and nurses there took good care of me, but they also couldn't quite figure out exactly what was wrong with me, and thus, couldn't figure out how to treat my illness. So I just spent all my time in the hospital, getting sicker. And because I was allergic to everything, I wasn't allowed to go *anywhere*.

I was stuck. The doctors put me in an isolation ward with six beds; I had the bed closest to the window. The first week I was there, the kid in the bed closest to the door died. A week later, the kid in the second bed died. About a month after that, the kid in the *third* bed died. At that point, the rest of us got together in the bathroom for a secret meeting, where we figured out what was going on. They had us in there *in order*.

If you think that was scary to me, you should have seen the face of the kid in bed number *four*.

The thing was, we were all pretty sick, and I sat up late that night, thinking about that, and about the friends I'd barely known and lost, and I realized something significant: none of us knows how much time we have in this world, in this life. I thought, Well, if we're in here in order, then I've got *maybe* a month. Maybe two. I don't want to waste any time—I may not have any time to waste! I want to start doing what I want to do right now. I don't want to wait until I'm older, because this may be all the life that I have.

That was both a profound and terrifying thing to realize.

I still wasn't allowed to leave my room—or at least, the floor it was on—and I started going a little stir-crazy. Accomplices were enlisted, and shenanigans ensued. Finally, the doctors gave in and offered me a compromise: One day a week I could go downstairs to the gift shop and browse. Now, if you're eleven years old and stuck in a hospital, being allowed to browse the gift shop isn't that enticing. For one thing, half of it was nothing but *flowers,* so I couldn't even *go* to that part of the shop. Most of the other half was all "get well" cards. And it's depressing to read lots of "get well" cards when you're not getting well, you don't know if you *will* get well, and you can't actually leave the hospital.

But the gift shop also had books, and magazines, and a comic book spinner rack. And I *loved* comic books. As a matter of fact, I had become a passionate collector of comic books. I had always read them—*Richie Rich, Archie,* and the Whitman Disney comics—but it was in the hospital that I became seriously addicted to superhero comics. I loved them all, and I bought them all: *Superman, Batman, Wonder Woman, Teen Titans*. My weekly trips downstairs to buy comic books at the gift shop became the one highlight in my life.

It was about this time that the doctors began telling my mother, "We don't know what's making him sick. And we don't know how to make him better. He's just getting worse. It may end up being the best thing for you to take him home and make him comfortable." That came as a bit of a shock to her—and to me. I was listening from the next room. At age eleven, I had just heard the doctors tell my mother that I was probably going to die. It's one thing to think it; it's something else to hear a doctor say it. That was a lot of weight for a kid to bear.

Then, the next Wednesday, the magazine vendor brought something else in with the comic books. They brought in a little paperback book that I bought, and which, all these years later, I still have. The book was called *Superman: Last Son of Krypton,* and it was by a writer named Elliot S! Maggin. He was supposed to write the book to go along with the Superman movie, but Elliot didn't actually write a book that had anything to do with the movie. And it wasn't your typical Superman story, either. He had written a lot of Superman comic books, but for the novel he basically wrote a very moral, virtuous, humanistic tale about a character who is trying to figure out what his place is in the world. I can still (almost) quote several passages from memory.

One particular passage involved young Clark Kent and his adoptive father, Jonathan Kent. Jonathan was dying, and he called his son to his bedside and said he had some things to tell his son. And Clark listened "for he believed the old man to be wiser than he."

Jonathan told him that a man is someone who assumes responsibility, and that to help people in need is right. He had taught his son one great fundamental truth: that there was a right and a wrong in the Universe, and the difference was not hard to distinguish. The message inherent throughout the book was make the right choices for the right reasons. That was an important thing for a dying father to be conveying to his son.

Those words resonated very strongly with me because earlier that year, I had received a letter from my grandfather, who helped to raise me after my father left. The letter was essentially a list of the things he wanted me to know about how I should live my life, the things he believed were most true.

Then, farther on in the Superman book, there was something else that resonated even more strongly. There was a scene where Superman had been interrogated by an enemy from another galaxy, and he was dying. It was like he was sick in almost the same way that I was sick, there in that hospital, and he began having fever dreams.

In the dreams, his father, Jor-El, came to him and told him that he might, in fact, be dying, and that maybe he would die—but it would be *his choice.* He told his son that he was meant to lead an extraordinary life, and that he was strong enough to overcome his challenges. Then he told him something that stunned me as I read it, there in my bed. He told his son that it was not merely his choice when he would die . . .

. . . But also whether he would die *at all.*

Jor-El told his son that he had the ability to choose his own destiny, and that his destiny was intertwined with the destiny of everyone else he touched; every life in the galaxy was connected to his. But he could choose either way. There would be no real benefit to himself, nothing to gain in heaven, in hell, or on earth, however he chose—save for the peace and freedom of his fellow beings.

If he chose to let go and die, his pain would be over, and he would be at peace.

If he chose to live, his life would be a never-ending battle against those who would do harm to the Universe— but he would get to be Superman.

That message was also very, very clear to me.

After one particularly painful weekend, I commented to a doctor, "Well, at least *that's* over." He very gently, but bluntly, told me that with my condition, it would never be "over." I could expect some kind of pain, some kind of discomfort, some kind of physical suffering, all my life.

That's when I realized that I was being given the same opportunity to choose that Kal-El was. I could decide to live. If I did, it would be difficult. It would be *hard*.

But it would be worth it, because I would get to be like Superman. And like him, my life could affect every other life I touched, and, like him, I would try to make the right choices and help everyone I could, because that's what Superman does.

The message Jor-El taught his son in that fever dream is one that applies to us all. We are all, each and every one, unique in the Universe. And that uniqueness makes us valuable.

I thought I understood that concept, but I don't think I really truly believed it until I had an experience that engraved it in my heart and soul. It was an experience that showed me how valuable one person's belief in another can be.

At the same time that I was in Good Samaritan Hospital, my grandfather was in Mesa Lutheran suffering from a heart condition. A few weeks after I read *Superman: Last Son of Krypton,* my grandfather called my mother and said he needed to see me, urgently. He said he needed to give me a father's blessing—something both significant and sacred in the church to which we belonged.

The family and doctors demurred, saying that neither of us was really well enough to leave at that time, even temporarily, but my grandfather held firm. It was necessary, he said. And so arrangements were made for both of us to get a day pass, and we met at my grandparents' house where my grandfather laid his hands upon my head to give me a blessing.

The words he spoke were not those I expected to hear: words about comfort and healing. Instead, he spoke very directly to me about the circumstances of my life in that moment.

"You get to choose," he said, "because I believe that you have a greater destiny than this. You get to choose how long you will be here, in this life." Without knowing it, at least on a purely physical level, his words mirrored those from the book I had already decided would change the course of my life.

He continued. "Choosing a long life does not mean the pain is over," he said solemnly. "You are going to have a difficult life, if that is what you choose. But it will be difficult because you are going to have a lot of gifts, and your voice will have the ability to move the hearts of men. If you're not strong enough, that's all right, too. But if you choose to do this, you're going to change the lives of millions of people. The words you speak will influence everyone who hears them, if you so choose, and if you live a good and honorable life."

He spoke for only a few more minutes, and other things were said. There were admonishments to help my mother and to take care of my siblings. But there were also promises that he and my grandmother loved me deeply, and that they believed in me and would always, always, be there for me when I needed them—no matter what. Promises that they would never let me fall.

After he went to such great lengths to give me that blessing, I knew what he had written in that letter to me was true. And more, I believed everything he said in that blessing to the core of my being. I believed that our Creator had given us a purpose in this life, and that I was being given the opportunity to choose whether to fulfill mine. Before the blessing was over, I was fully resolved in my love for my grandfather and in his for me, and I was not going to let him down.

When he had finished, he hugged and kissed me, and we went back to our respective hospitals. Not long after that, he died. Somehow, he had known what was coming, and that knowledge had fueled his urgency. He somehow knew he was going to have fewer opportunities to say those important things to me, and writing that letter and voicing that blessing were how he chose to seize those opportunities.

In *Superman: Last Son of Krypton,* a dying father taught his son what it meant to be a man, and a dying son learned of his great destiny and of his power to choose. There in the Good Samaritan Hospital, a dying grandfather taught his grandson what it meant to be a man, and a dying boy made a choice that changed his life.

Sometimes we see and recognize signs along our path that tell us we are going in the right direction. I call that Synchronicity. But when others are drawn to us to help confirm the meaning and significance of those signs, I believe it is Guidance. A way for us to choose how to find the way to our purpose, and a way for us to use our gifts to serve that purpose.

The lesson I learned during my time in the hospital is one of the most important messages I share, and one of the most important things I can tell someone who is struggling: *You have a greater destiny than this.* You are meant for greater things than this. And if you want to beat this, to overcome whatever it is you're grappling with, *you are strong enough to do it.* And if that's the choice you make, it's possible to live a wonderful, extraordinary life.

If you don't think you're strong enough, that's okay too. Everyone gets to choose what they can bear. Choosing that is a fundamental right, which no one else can judge. And sometimes, choosing to live is very, very hard. But I promise you, you *are* strong enough—if you want to be.

You have a greater destiny than this. And it's always there to be chosen.

I slept with that Superman book under my pillow for *months*. And as I read, and reread, and *re-reread* that book, an idea began to form. The doctors didn't know what was wrong with me, and they didn't know how to help. But maybe, just maybe, their diagnosis was *wrong*. Maybe getting better was going to be up to *me*.

Working with another doctor, I started something

she called Adjunct Therapy—today, we call it creative visualization—where I started imagining and visualizing my favorite superheroes shrinking down and going into my bloodstream where they began destroying all the bad blood cells, fixing the good ones, and basically trying to believe myself better.

As I did this—an hour every morning and an hour every night—I had another breakthrough idea, also inspired by another Elliot S! Maggin story I read in a DC Comics digest I bought in the gift shop. In that story, Superman had been thrown into a strange world where all his powers had been drained, leaving him weakened. But in the course of the story, he realized that the same rules which took his strength could return it as well. All he had to do was choose it, and his strength and powers would return.

Pain, I realized, was only a temporary condition; it was nothing more than weakness leaving my body. And I could *choose* to take back my strength. My choice was augmented by something even more powerful: my grandfather's belief in me. When someone in whom you trust completely says that they believe in you, you find yourself drawing on physical and spiritual reserves you didn't realize you possessed. Your will is strengthened. And your purpose manifests itself in powerful ways.

Suddenly, something unexpected began to happen. I started to get *better*. I got better enough that the doctors told my mother she could take me home, but to bring me back the next week, just in case. Weeks away from the hospital became months, and eventually, I didn't have to go back at all.

To this day, I still have allergies and migraines. I still have to carry an epi-pen for a possible allergic reaction (which is better than the syringe that I used to have to use!). But I've never again been as sick as I was that year. To remind myself of the lessons I learned and the choices I made, I still wear a Superman ring.

One of the compelling thoughts I took from that experience is that none of us knows how much time we have in this life. I had enough experiences in the hospital with friends who were there one night and had passed away the next that I realized there was no time to waste. The time we have is all we get. That inspired an absolutely maniacal drive to start doing what I wanted to do with my life *immediately*. To seize my purpose and embrace my great destiny. What I decided I wanted to do was write and draw comics. In that moment, my life changed and my career began.

Be so good they can't ignore you.

STEVE MARTIN

CHAPTER THREE

QUALITY IS WHAT MATTERS MOST

My aunt, who was a professional graphic designer, took me as her apprentice when I was about thirteen. In between doing cleanup work on her projects and finishing my first pro logo design (for Hatch Construction & Paving, which they still use today), she helped me start preparing portfolios to send to the comic book companies. I wrote a cover letter to go with them, which basically said, "Here I am, your next great discovery. I'd really love to start on *Justice League,* but if you need to ease me into things by starting me on *Batman,* that's okay, too."

They would send my portfolios back, usually with a form rejection letter. Every once in a while, an editor would actually look at what I sent them, and send me back something a little more elaborate, but they all said the same thing: Maybe when you're older. Maybe after high school. Maybe after college. But not now—you're just too *young*.

I understood the editors' points of view, but I didn't agree with it, and I wasn't shy about saying so. My age should not have mattered at *all*. The only thing that should have mattered was whether I could do the job I was applying for, and do it well.

This is one of my favorite messages to share with kids: that I believe they can do anything they choose to do in this life, and it doesn't matter how old they are. All that matters is if they have the desire and determination to put in the effort required to be good at what they do.

When people question this idea, I casually ask them to look at the ages of most world-class gymnasts. Age is irrelevant, and youth dominates the field.

In my own creative field, though, I still had a lot to learn. I wasn't really at a professional level yet with my writing or art. But I had the ambition, and I had the desire. I had a goal, and I was willing to keep working to improve my craft. So I kept sending the packages—and I kept getting rejection letters. Then one day, I came across something new and unique in the world of comics: a large, oversized, black-and-white magazine-shaped comic book called *ElfQuest*.

I liked fantasy already, but what intrigued me was the story behind the story. The book was created by a husband and wife team—and in her case, a working professional artist—who had been rejected by all the same publishers I'd been approaching for work. When no one wanted to publish their quirky fantasy comic, they borrowed some money and set up their own publishing company.

And suddenly, *ElfQuest* became a smashing success, and was for a time, one of the darlings of the comics industry. They were selling 80,000 copies per issue of the black-and-white comics, and the first color album—which was one of the first graphic novels to be carried in the major bookstores outside the comics market—sold a *million* copies.

This got, and kept, my attention. And my focus changed: I wasn't interested (as much) in just working for a comic book company. I would start my own, and publish work I created.

I created a new portfolio of original work and talked my aunt into driving me to the World Science Fiction convention in Anaheim where the *ElfQuest* creators were hosting a party.

It was the first big convention that I'd ever been to, and while there were a lot of things to do and see, my main purpose was to meet the people who had inspired me. And, being all of fourteen, I was scared to death.

At the party, after sweating blood for three hours walking around and getting up the nerve to actually approach them, I finally showed them the portfolio of work I'd created. They seemed impressed—a gentle act of mercy, for the work was good but not great—and said it was all very nice, but they weren't taking on any new books.

I replied that I wasn't interested in them publishing my book. They said they weren't making any investments. I said I didn't want them to invest in me. They said they weren't hiring any new artists either. I said that was okay, that I didn't want them to hire me. A bit flustered and slightly rattled, they finally asked me why I had come all that way to show them my portfolio if I wasn't asking to be published, invested in, or hired.

I said, "I wanted to show this to you so you would know who I was. Because you inspired me. I'm going to do what you did. I'm going to start my own publishing company. And the next time you see me, it will be as your colleague."

Of course, their reaction was similar to everyone

else's—that it was good to be ambitious, but I was too young. Maybe when I was older. But not now.

I thanked them for their time, spilled ice cream on a famous comics writer on my way out of the party (who is now my pal, Len Wein), and we left the convention.

Back home in Arizona, I sat down with my best friend and decided we were smart enough to figure out how to start a publishing company. First, we decided we needed to start a comic book store.

One thing that came out of that discussion was the fact we spent a *lot* of money on comics. But if we got a tax license like a business, we could get our comic books wholesale. Just like businesses did.

In fact, it could *be* a business.

We'd buy our comics for half off, which would save us a lot of hard-earned paper route money, and if we bought extras and sold *those,* we'd earn more profits, all of which could go into a war chest to start a publishing company. He thought that was a great idea. So we toasted with ginger ale and got to work.

We arranged to rent an old grocery store for eighty bucks a month and planned to sell comic books, Louis L'Amour western paperbacks, and corn nuts, because those were the three products we could get wholesale accounts for.

Pretty quickly, we realized we couldn't really run a comic book store successfully while we were still going to school during the day, especially since I was spending nights writing and drawing comic book pages. There was also the matter of things like utilities, and having to restock the corn nuts. Eventually, we bailed on the storefront idea and instead talked my mother into giving us the back end of her house where we could set up our operation as a mail-order service.

We took over the three back rooms—consisting of my bedroom, the studio room, and the business office—and began creating a monthly catalog through which we could keep selling comic books every month. Slowly, we started saving up money, but another realization hit home: even if we had the money to publish the comic I was creating, there was no way to really promote and market it.

No promotion meant no sales—and that wasn't quite what we had in mind for our grand destiny. We had to figure out a way to tell people what we had for sale. Then one day, a revelation: We needed to be exhibitors at the San Diego comic book convention, the largest comics convention in the country. It was a great, even thrilling idea, and one that was going to take a lot more money than we had.

So, at the age of fifteen, we decided we needed to get ourselves a bank loan.

We started approaching bankers, beginning with the ones we could reach on our bicycles. One thought drove us, the idea that I mentioned at the beginning of this book: If you really want to do something, no one can stop you; but if you really don't want to do something, then no one can help you. But the choice is always entirely up to you.

We'd written up a business plan for the convention, which we dutifully presented to each bank we approached. Unsurprisingly, the bankers had the same response that all of the editors with the publishing companies had, which is that we were very ambitious, but too young. I started to think the phrase "Maybe when you're older" was something being passed around in secret by everyone over the age of twenty.

So we thanked them for their time, and kept trying. And we kept getting turned down. I think we approached thirty-two different bankers—all the ones we could talk our parents to driving us to—until my pal got his license and he could drive us himself. We even started asking private businessmen about possible corporate sponsorships, but every one of them said no.

At one point, I had even started hitting up bankers in other states. I talked my mother into driving us to the Petrified Forest, via Holbrook, then distracted her so she wouldn't see the road signs pointing to New Mexico. She was utterly confused as to how that had happened—until I helpfully offered to go into a bank to ask for directions, and she suddenly realized why I had worn my Sunday clothes on a field trip. That bank turned us down, too.

We'd nearly run out of options when one of the last bankers we approached, who was actually the new manager at the bank closest to my home (and thus, hadn't technically turned us down himself) agreed to a meeting.

He listened to our presentation, then said, "I like you boys. I like what I see in your eyes. I like what I hear in your voices. I think I'm going to give you this loan."

To this day, we're pretty sure the money came out of his own pocket and not the bank because we got another loan a year later and there was a lot more paperwork involved. But that day, there was one piece of paper that said basically that we promised to repay the loan. That was it.

He gave us the loan, and we signed up for an exhibitor's booth at Comic-Con and the trade show which ran with it. We built backdrops and displays out of pegboards and molding in my mother's barnyard, and we arranged the printing of the completed comic book I'd written and drawn.

We talked my long-suffering aunt into driving the U-Haul truck we needed in order to transport the displays and all the comics; neither one of us was old enough to rent a truck ourselves. We paid for a hotel room, in advance, which turned out to be a good thing.

The U-Haul didn't run all that well across the desert, and we arrived late in San Diego only to find that our hotel, the stately old U.S. Grant, had given away our room— our *prepaid* room. So they gave us the only thing they had left: the Presidential Suite.

We had stopped at the printer's on the way and picked up ten thousand copies of my first comic book, which we called *Pryderi Terra*. It was magazine-sized like *ElfQuest* had been, and it had a lot of flaws. Overall, it was still a fairly semi-amateur production. I obviously still had a lot to learn about writing and drawing, but I had actually produced and published a full comic book. And parts of it—just parts, not all—were really, really good.

At the convention itself we learned something really interesting. This was a quarter-century ago, in the days when Comic-Con wasn't quite the big media event it is now with pirate ships and Batmobiles and all those other huge, extravagant things. Back then, everybody had a ten-foot booth. Everybody had the same tables. So DC Comics, a huge corporation, had a ten-foot booth where they had their Superman posters, their Batman comics, and their Wonder Woman T-shirts on display.

Across the aisle was Marvel Comics, with their X-Men comics, and their Fantastic Four T-shirts, and their Hulk posters on display.

And then there was us—me, my best friend, our other friend Bryan, and a graphic designer—with our T-shirts, and our art prints, and our comic books spread out across the displays we'd built in my mother's barnyard.

The convention opened their doors, and the fans came in and started buying stuff from Marvel, and from DC, and from us.

I suddenly realized that it didn't matter to all those people walking by that we were basically a small company, a small publisher. It didn't matter to them that we were teenagers who couldn't drive a stick shift. All that mattered to them was that we had this *thing* on the table, something that we had produced, that had *quality.* Quality that they were willing to pay money for.

In that moment, we were just as powerful as every other company there. All those big companies that told us we were too young didn't matter anymore, because we had proven it could be done. Nothing else mattered to the attendees—only the quality of our work was important. Just that.

And nobody cared how old we were.

There were still difficult moments—like realizing we'd printed the books on an expensive paper, which raised the unit cost to five cents per copy more than our wholesale price—and just being present at the Con wasn't always enough. But you use the resources you have—and I had panache and a suite at the U.S. Grant.

If a retailer seemed hesitant to purchase copies for his store, I'd tell him not to decide then, but to come over to my suite for drinks so we could discuss it further.

Later, they'd show up at my door at the U.S. Grant, looking like they were about to be arrested just for being there. I'd invite them in, ask if they preferred sitting in the living room or the dining room, and offer them a choice of 7-Up or Dr. Pepper. They'd sit there the whole time wondering how the blazes I was paying for that suite while I persuaded them to stock my comics in their stores.

We ended up selling enough to pay off the loan and

did fairly well, overall. But I realized I still had a *whole* lot more to learn about publishing. So we went back home and got to work. I kept working on my comic book stories, but I started doing other kinds of work, including commercial work, to keep learning new techniques. My friend Bryan, our other Comic-Con veteran, helped me improve my writing. And I immersed myself in business books, to learn more about running a company as quickly as I could. But I never forgot the lessons I learned going to San Diego that year.

You have to put in the effort to do quality work, because that's what will matter most. Because if the quality is there, *no one* will care how old you are.

Destiny is not a matter of chance;
it is a matter of choice;
it is not a thing to be waited for,
it is a thing to be achieved.

WILLIAM JENNINGS BRYAN

Circumstance does not make the man;
it reveals him.

JAMES ALLEN

PART II

Live deliberately.

Decide:
Are you the kind of
person things happen to,
or the kind of person
who makes things happen?

Dare he, for whom circumstances make it possible to realize his true destiny, refuse it simply because he is not prepared to give up everything else?

Dag Hammarskjold

CHAPTER FOUR

SOMETIMES, A CATASTROPHE IS ONLY A COURSE CORRECTION

I finished high school and moved to the Phoenix area, where I started up a studio that focused on doing commercial work—which largely meant I was doing pot pie ads for the local grocery store, and taking impossible jobs like trying to design a female Sun Devil for ASU so they could market a new line of women's clothing. (Did. Not. Work.)

I eventually started doing design work for large companies and publishers, and even film studios. (I'll be clear: the work was still of the "draw a pot pie" variety, except for the occasional thrilling design job, which happened once in a blue moon.) But I wasn't really doing what I'd always aspired to be doing. Somehow, in my pursuit of better skills, I'd lost track of the very work I wanted to apply those skills to doing. I'd moved away from the storytelling that I loved.

I'd moved away from comics. Which was bad.

The reason that was bad was that I had moved away from what I loved the most; I'd taken my eye off the true prize. One of my mentors, the philosopher Larry Austin, once told me that it was easy to see putting your hand on a hot stove as a bad idea, and ultimately harmful. But something that doesn't create immediate pain can cause harm nonetheless. And nothing can be as painful as moving away from something you love and not even realizing you've done it.

I focused on the work I was doing that was paying the bills (and sometimes, not). I got married, and my studio got larger. I had a few opportunities and a few setbacks—some of which were better learning experiences than the opportunities were—but I hadn't really figured out the direction I was supposed to be going. I hadn't quite figured out what my grand destiny was supposed to be.

Then, from out of the blue, I was offered a great opportunity. I got a phone call from a friend of mine who told me about a great job opening that was about to be available at the Sullivan Bluth Studio. This was the animation studio run by Don Bluth, who made (among other films) *All Dogs Go to Heaven, The Secret of NIMH,* and *An American Tail.* All great animated movies that I loved. My friend told me that the studio was about to start hiring storyboard artists, and if I wanted in, I should get to the studio and snap up that job, because with my comics experience (all two issues, not counting portfolios) I'd be perfect for it.

A storyboard artist is the person who takes the script for a movie and lays out the scenes in pictures on one wall so that everyone working on the film can see every aspect of the story from start to finish. So basically, *comics.* It's telling one big story, as a comic strip, on the wall.

And I thought, I can *do* that. I would *love* to do that. This is the ideal job for me—and perhaps my great destiny. I asked my friend what I would need to do to get this job, and he told me that the job opening wasn't public, so all I really needed to do was walk in and ask for it.

At the Sullivan Bluth Studio.

In Dublin.

As in, Dublin, *Ireland*—where the studio was based.

That was a bit of a big choice to be making. A big move. I hemmed and hawed over it for a few months. I went back and forth over the possibility, wondering, is this something we can really *do?* Can we do this? I finally decided this was the right choice, this was the option, this was the grand destiny, here, being handed to me if only I'd be bold enough to take it. And so my wife and I made the decision to do it. There was just one problem: we'd only been married four months, and we didn't have the money to move to Ireland. But destiny awaited—so we had a yard sale.

We basically got together with some friends and sold almost everything we had. Clothes, utensils, furniture, pots and pans, the dog dish (although we kept the dog). Basically everything that could be sold was sold, except for my book collection, the drafting table my mother had given me when I was eight, my wife's sewing machine, and the hope chest that her grandfather had made for her.

Everything else was gone by evening.

Somehow, we raised enough money for a plane ticket and one night in a bed-and-breakfast, which was enough to get me to Ireland and get started. My wife went to go stay with her family, the dog went to go stay with my mother, and we put the last things we owned in storage. Then I got on a plane for Ireland with a suitcase, a brief-case, and a portfolio.

Dublin is a fascinating city, in part because it's a thousand years old. You can sit on a bench in the middle

of Phoenix Park—one of the largest urban parks in the
world—and look down over all the centuries-old steeples
rising up out of the fog. Down by the base of the park,
next to the River Liffey, was the Sullivan Bluth Studio,
where Don Bluth and his crew made all those great animated movies.

I sat there on that bench, and looked over the mag-
nificent scene in front of me, and thought, this is *perfect*.
This *is* my great destiny. To be here, living in this place. To
be able to work with these artists who are so inspiring to
me, whom I've admired for so long. To do the kind of work
that I was always meant to do. *This* is what I'm supposed
to be doing.

That was a truth that, in that moment, I believed with
all my heart.

I went down to the studio, told them who I was, and
what job I was there for. They said, "Great! Let's show you
around and introduce you to a few people." They gave me
a tour of the studio, which was spectacular. Every room
was full of wonderful art—all of the designs for every
movie that they'd done, side by side with art from the
movies they were currently working on, movies that *I'd*
soon be working on.

After visiting their warehouse down the road where

they kept all the art archives, I met some more of the artists and a few of the supervisors. I told them which job I was there for, and my friend had been right. They had been hiring for those positions, but hadn't gotten any other applicants. Apparently, my inside track had been well-informed. I told them who referred me—which got me some curious looks, and which I might have taken as fore-shadowing had I been paying more attention—and I gave them my qualifications and my portfolio, and basically said I was ready to get to work.

A supervisor put me in a room, gave me a studio news-letter to read, and told me to hold tight, someone would come along in a little while for orientation and to get me settled in.

They left me there, in that little room, for *six hours*.

Finally, at the end of my wits, somebody came along, stuck their head in the door, and said, "Are you James Owen?" I said I was. He told me that there was a meeting going on, and I should follow him. That's the point at which I found out everything *else* that was going on at the studio.

They had been having a series of huge meetings where they were gathering together a bunch of the artists to tell them the bad news, which was that the studio had just lost all of their bank financing for the next *five projects*. Eventually, the whole studio might have to be shut down. This was a process that had already been in the works for some time, and worse, they were only going to be able to keep people on staff based on seniority for the projects already in progress. Everyone else was going to be let go.

I had been there for six hours.

What's more, all this may have already been happening when I first found out about the storyboarding job; my fear was confirmed when they told me they were not even hiring for the jobs that had been open. They had been letting artists go to tighten their belts, but keeping the hiring channels open to appease their connections to the Irish Arts groups that had backed them initially. The friend that had told me about the job opening was no longer at the studio, or even still living in Ireland.

It became more and more clear that the Sullivan Bluth Studio was in the process of shutting down. Some months after my ill-fated trip, they *did* shut down the entire studio, but all I was concerned about that day was the fact that I walked out of that studio without the job I'd moved to Ireland to take.

I walked up the hill, into the park to the same bench where I had been sitting earlier. I sat down, stuck my hand in my pocket, and realized that one coin, one Irish pound, was all the money I had left in the world. And that was it, and that was all.

I thought, how did this happen to me? Six hours ago, everything was *perfect*. Everything was ideal. This was my grand destiny. And suddenly, everything was a *disaster*. How did this happen? I thought I was the kind of person that made things happen, not the kind of person things happened *to*.

As that thought struck me, I realized something: We have to *choose* to live deliberately. Things are going to happen to us whether we make choices or not. So it's up to us to make the choices to make things happen. To be the kind of people who make things happen, not the kind of people things happen to. We have to choose to live deliberately. To actually *actively* make choices.

I also realized something very profound: we get to make little choices, relatively inconsequential choices, all the time, but we get the chance to make those choices that might change our entire future very few times in our lives—and I had before me an extraordinary opportunity. The very next choice I made would determine my *entire* future. It would shape the entire course of my life. That is a rare and meaningful gift. It would have been almost thrilling if I hadn't been freezing to death on that bench.

The last time I had made such a choice had been just over a decade earlier, sitting in the Good Samaritan Hospital. Since that time, I had been searching for what my true mission in life was supposed to be, the path that would allow me to do what I loved and still find ways to influence people and help change their lives for the better.

I had accomplished a few of the things I had set out to do, but at twenty-two years old, I was still basically just a boy who hadn't done anything yet. Everything that came before that moment when I found myself on that bench in Ireland was just learning; even the recovery from my childhood illness had been a process. But this—*this* was a *moment*; a single moment to make a life-altering decision.

That was when I grew up.

I looked at that Irish pound and considered my options. An Irish pound, which is worth about a buck and a half, is not much to go on, but I decided it would somehow be enough, and I made my choice.

I went down the hill to a pay phone and I called my wife—collect—and I told her I had some good news and some bad news. The bad news was that we weren't moving to Ireland. I explained that some things had happened that I'd tell her about later, but the good news was that I'd decided to start a new publishing company. I didn't need a studio; I didn't need a staff. All I needed was some paper, and pens, and pencils, and I'd go back to doing what I should have been doing all along: my comic books.

I've said this a couple of times, and I'll repeat it again before we're done: If you really, really want to do something, no one can stop you. But if you really *don't* want to do something, then no one can help you. But I believe that if you make that hard decision, to do that thing you want to do most, people will see it in your face. They'll hear it in your voice, and they will find ways to help you.

This is another one of those great truths about how we respond to one another as creative beings. If you whine, and moan, and lament your bad luck, people might commiserate with you—but they aren't likely to feel compelled to help. On the other hand, if your response to a bad circumstance is to form a plan, and smile, and insist that somehow, despite the obstacles, you *will* find a way to make things work, then people see that, and they'll respond to it. And you'll have more help than you believed possible.

I told everyone I knew what my plan was, to start this new company, and my news—and enthusiasm—began to spread. Friends I had made there—who knew how little money I had and who knew what was happening over at the studio—heard what I was choosing to do. They knew I didn't have a job and that a lot of other people were about to be out of *their* jobs. My response to the situation, which was that I was going to start a company with no money, slightly befuddled them. Still, they helped me out and made sure I had enough to eat while I worked out what would happen next.

And someone whom I had never met (and haven't still, to this day), someone from my church, who was in Galway on the other side of Ireland, heard about my situation and decided I needed a hand. He called the bed-and-breakfast where I was staying, told them who he was, and said if they would let me stay as long as I needed to stay and feed me whatever I needed to eat, then whenever I ended up needing to leave, he'd come in and settle the bill.

And they agreed.

It was also a profound sense of comfort to me that among the art which lined the hallway to the foyer of the bed-and-breakfast was a large print of *The Angelus,* a quiet scene of farmers praying in a field, which had been painted by Jean Millet.

Then another serendipitous, synchronous lucky break

happened. It turned out that a round-trip ticket to Ireland had been cheaper than a one-way ticket, so we had arranged for a return flight (eight days later) that I'd never planned to use.

I had a place to stay, food to eat, and a ticket home. I spent my days in my room, watching U2 videos and forming a plan for my new company. And at the end of that week, I flew home.

I had been convinced that this job, and living in that beautiful place, was my great destiny. The truth is, even if I had been able to stay, I'd have eventually lost the job anyway when the studio closed for good. At least the way things happened, I was able to realize what I really wanted wasn't in Ireland, and wasn't at that company, sooner rather than later. What seemed to be a catastrophe was merely a course correction. And I was headed home to find my true destiny.

I had a suitcase, a briefcase, a portfolio, one Irish Pound, a plan, and the determination to somehow see it through and make it work.

If you really, really want to do something, that's all you need.

*You can have everything in life
you want, if you will just help enough
other people get what they want.*

Zig Ziglar

He who would accomplish little
must sacrifice little;
he who would achieve much
must sacrifice much;
he who would attain highly
must sacrifice greatly.

JAMES ALLEN

CHAPTER FIVE

IF YOU REALLY WANT IT, NO REASON IS BIG ENOUGH TO STOP YOU

I spent that week in Ireland, then came back to Arizona, where my wife and I moved into a little apartment. We had a book collection, a drafting table, a sewing machine, a hope chest, and a dog—and nothing else. She got a job selling floor coverings to pay the bills while I worked on the comics. When she got her first check, we bought some paper, pens, and pencils. With those art supplies, I started drawing what would become the first issue of my comic book series called *StarChild*.

This was an amalgam of stories that I had wanted to do since very early in my career. I'd started a Superman story years before, which is where the title came from: StarChild is Kal-El in Kryptonese.

The main story came from an adaptation of *Silas*

Marner by George Eliot that I was doing for a company called Classics Illustrated, which, according to a now-familiar pattern, started to go under not long after contracting me for the book. (And incidentally, that story is why the main character in *StarChild* is an old weaver hermit. He was originally Silas Marner; I just changed him into my character, Ezekiel Higgins, so the sixteen pages I'd already drawn wouldn't be wasted.)

I'd run a comic book company before, so I knew how to do it and I knew what my obstacles were. The main goal was to sell enough copies to pay for the printing bill. If we could pay for the printing bill, then I could work on the next issues. That way I could build an audience while my wife's job could take care of the bills at home.

To pay for a minimum three thousand copy print run, which was the lowest you could do, economically speaking, we had to sell at least a thousand copies right off the bat. I finished that first issue of *StarChild,* and we sent it into the catalogs. A few months later, we got back orders for twelve hundred copies, which was ideal. We'd covered the printing bill *and* had pizza money left over. Priorities, you know.

The second issue came out a month later, on time, but the numbers were a different story. The orders came in for only six hundred copies. That was a little bit of a problem. If we couldn't pay the printing bill, we couldn't go on to issue number three, or four, or five—and my career would be over before it had even started. But then something happened that changed *everything*.

One week after the second issue of *StarChild* shipped to the comic book stores, I crushed my drawing hand in a car accident.

A young lady made a left-hand turn in front of me when I had a green light. I plowed into her, and my hand plowed into the radio. I shattered the bones in my first two fingers, and badly bruised my knuckles. At the hospital, the doctors examined my hand and said there was too much damage to do surgery, which would just create scar tissue. The best they could do was put the bones in place, let them set, and then send me to therapy for a year. But, at best, they said I was going to probably only get thirty to forty percent usage of my hand again.

For the second time that year, I had a big decision to make. I had to decide how much I really wanted to do what I was doing, because according to the doctors, my career as an artist was all but over. For my part, I believed something different. I believed that if you really want to do something, no one can stop you, but if you really don't want to do something, no one can help you.

Picture the situation: My hand was in a brace from my fingertips to my elbow. After the initial shock had worn off, I announced I was going to rehabilitate my hand, heal completely, and then pick up where I'd left off with issue three of *StarChild*.

And everyone in the world decided I was *wrong*.

The doctors, my friends, my family, and a few curious patients all gathered around me and basically said that they appreciated the fact that I was trying to be optimistic about what had happened, and that having a positive attitude was a good thing. But they also insisted that I needed to be *realistic*. I needed to accept what had happened to me. Everything had changed, and I was not going to be able to do what I used to do.

These were people who cared about me, who loved me, that were saying these things. I had a hard decision to make.

There's something I want to stress that I hope you'll keep in mind: I believe *every one of us* has something that's very unique to us specifically. Something unique enough that no one else might really ever understand it. Not our parents, or teachers, or best friends, or siblings.

It's our point of view.

Our point of view is what makes us unique, because no one else—*no one else*—has your particular combination of thoughts, and dreams, and hopes, and desires, and ambitions, and memories, and experiences. No one. And I believe that every once in a while, the Universe opens itself up to you—and *you alone*—and shows you something that no one else is going to understand. You have to decide in that moment how much you believe in what you have seen. Even if everyone else in the world tells you you're wrong.

Does it help to have people who share your vision and believe in your grand destiny? Of course. But that isn't always how things work out. Sometimes you find yourself facing your Dragons all alone, and you have to choose, not in ignorance, but with the full understanding you have. And you have to accept the responsibility for the fact that it may be an irrevocable choice. From that moment forward, everything may change, but no one can decide to take that step except you.

So I made my choice. I politely and respectfully explained to everyone in my life, and everyone else in the world, thank you, but you're wrong. I'm an artist, and this is what I *do*. And somehow, I'm going to find a way to keep doing what I do. I'm going to keep doing my comic books. I'm going to keep writing—and drawing—*StarChild*.

I met with the therapist and explained my point of view.

"Listen," I told him, "I don't *need* to be able to open up peanut butter jars—my wife's really good at that. I don't *need* to be able to tie my own shoes. I don't even *need* to be able to dress myself—that's what Velcro and sweats are for. What I *need* to be able to do is hold a pen or pencil. That's all that I care about, and all I want to work on."

Thus, every day for the next eight months, either at home or down the street at the hospital, I worked with a therapist, who had me do the same thing over and over and over again for four hours a day: I would use my thumb and fingers to put screws into blocks of wood and then pull them out again. That's it. Performing that specific motion of putting those screws in and pulling them out again was meant to tighten and train those muscles to hold a pen again.

Then, after therapy, I would take a bus to Kinkos where I could rent a Macintosh computer for ten dollars an hour (or five dollars an hour if I waved at the employees with the brace). Working an hour at a time, I started typesetting pages for a story that I called *StarChild Number Zero,* which I designed as a prequel to issues one and two.

I couldn't letter it as I had the other comics, because my hand was in the brace. But I could typeset a story, and I had designed *StarChild Number Zero* to have a half-page illustration on one side of each page, and a half-page of text on the other. I knew I could still write my comics, and I could still design them. I just couldn't *draw* them.

That's when I figured out the Secret.

If you hear a voice within you saying, "You are not a painter," then by all means paint . . . and that voice will be silenced.

Vincent van Gogh

INTERLUDE

THE SECRET
OF DRAWING

The secret of drawing is just two things. It's very simple. It's very Zen.

First, it's making lines on paper.
And second, it's choosing where they go.

That's it. That's the secret of drawing.

It sounds very simple, but think about it—every lousy drawing you've ever seen was made by somebody who made choices about where those lines went.

If you're an artist, and you've made a drawing that you're not happy with, think about that. You made every one of those lines. You made a choice every time you made a line. Your drawing is the sum of all those choices.

The only difference between a good drawing and a bad drawing is the choices you made while you were drawing it.

Slow down. Be more considerate about the choices you're making. Be deliberate about the lines you draw. Be as certain as you can be that you have chosen correctly. Then begin to draw. And keep drawing. If you're unsure about a line, then stop, and consider it further until you are.

It's very much the same in life: Make better choices. Make better lines. Live a better life.

Choices are inevitable—there's no way to avoid them. So—take a deep breath. Choose the line you want to make. And draw.

What you create from there is *entirely* up to you.

*There is a point at which
everything becomes simple and
there is no longer any question of
choice, because all you have staked
will be lost if you look back.
Life's point of no return.*

DAG HAMMARSKJOLD

CHAPTER SIX

YOU HAVEN'T LOST UNTIL YOU CHOOSE TO STOP

No one would have blamed me. That's the thought that kept resonating inside my head. No one would have blamed me if I had listened to the conventional wisdom and accepted the fact that I could no longer draw. I could still write, of course, but my identity, my *complete* identity, included being able to draw. So while the Secret of Drawing may seem to be both obvious and profound, that knowledge was definitely earned through trials of fire.

I couldn't make the lines I wanted to make with my right hand, but I *could* still make lines with my left hand. My right hand, damaged as it was, had the muscle memory. I just couldn't access it again, yet. But that wasn't where I was choosing—I was choosing which lines to make with my *mind*.

For *StarChild Number Zero*, I did all the half-page illustration layouts in pencil, with my left hand. It took a *lot* of time, and it involved a lot more patience and frustration than I ever imagined it would. It was a bit like taking a doctor and telling him he had to perform brain surgery with a dull rock. It's doable, but really hard. But I could still draw, because I could make the lines with one hand. And I was still making the choices about where those lines went.

The creative struggles weren't the only ones I had to deal with. My friend's insurance company agreed to take care of his car (the one I'd wrecked in the accident), and they agreed to pay for the hospital stay and for my therapy, but there would be no compensation for lost income.

"We called up some comic book stores," they told me, "and none of them had ever heard of James Owen or of *Starburst.*"

"You mean *StarChild*," I said.

"Yeah, whatever. Anyway, they've never heard of you. And besides, your own sales show a fifty percent drop between the first two issues. At that rate, you'd be out of business by issue five."

They concluded that my comics were a *hobby,* and not

a *career,* and they weren't going to pay a penny for my lost income.

The printer we'd used on the first two issues agreed to wait for payment until I could pull *StarChild Number Zero* together. That would still take months; I could pencil layouts left-handed, but I was nowhere near steady enough to be able to ink. In the meantime, my wife's income from the carpet store could sustain our living needs.

Then, two months into my therapy, she was laid off from her job.

Everything had just become much more urgent.

I needed a bigger hammer.

The general consensus among the comics industry—the parts who knew I existed—was "He had a lot of promise, but it's over now." The stores which had been supportive of *StarChild* continued to be. But we were running out of money and options very, very quickly. I realized that doing a stylized prequel to the first two issues wasn't going to be enough, even if I could finish it more quickly. It had to be an *event.*

Because I had begun my comics career years earlier with *Pryderi Terra,* I had gotten to know a number of other professionals in the field. And I still had their phone numbers. I started calling them up with a proposition, telling them what had happened to my hand, explaining that I needed help assembling this comic book, and asking if they'd be willing to ink a half-page layout.

StarChild Number Zero was turning into a benefit book—but I would only print the books in one edition, and never reprint it, so I wouldn't be making money forever off their generosity. I just needed to get back on my feet, so to speak. As an added incentive, I offered to donate all of the original art to a charity auction.

If you make it clear you are determined to do something, people see it in your face, and they hear it in your voice. And they find ways to help you.

My good friend Paul Chadwick, who created a remarkable series called *Concrete,* responded first, agreeing to do a page. Dave Sim, who later became a mentor to me, agreed to do one soon after, followed by the amazing Colleen Doran. Craig Russell, the Art Deco-influenced comics artist whom I admired greatly, came in at the behest of Craig Hamilton, who offered to do *two* pages.

The book was rapidly filling up with amazing guest artists, but none more amazing than the last: the great Will Eisner, who the industry awards at Comic-Con are named after. He was doing comic books in the 1930s, and was one of the great pioneers of the medium. And he agreed to do one of these illustrations with me. The legendary illustrator Kelly Freas offered to write an afterword, and author Alan Dean Foster, whom I had met at a local convention, agreed to write an introduction. It was shaping up to be an astonishing book.

All of these great artists began working on the illustrations while I continued my therapy and learned just how much I hate putting screws into blocks of wood. Our whole plan was to try to sell enough copies of *StarChild Number Zero* to pay for the remainder of the bill for issue two, to pay for its own printing bill, and to pay for the upcoming printing bill for issue number three. If we could do that, then we hoped to sell the remaining stock of the first two issues to cover our personal bills.

At that point, my hand was healing well enough that I could pencil and ink again—albeit still very slowly—so I was able to add bookend illustrations to the story. And when the last page came in, we assembled the book and prepared the catalog listing.

Coming from selling six hundred copies of issue two, I would have been thrilled if we could just sell the minimum three thousand copies. We put the issue in the catalogs and crossed our fingers.

Two months later, we got the initial orders.

We had sold thousands upon thousands of copies. Tens of thousands. Eventually, we sold almost the entirety of my very optimistically (read: *insanely*) estimated print run, which had been decided prior to orders, of *StarChild Number Zero*.

It became one of the best-selling independent comic books of that entire season. Every comic book store in the world now knew my name, in large part because of that list of contributors who had agreed to help me. My friends Colleen Doran, Dave Sim, Martin Wagner, and Jeff Smith asked if I wanted to spend the summer doing a promotional tour of all the conventions and industry trade shows with them.

And I finished issue number three—which sold seventeen thousand copies.

Eventually, a lawyer friend of ours who generously took the legal case for almost nothing (plus a hand-colored art print) *did* manage to procure a decent settlement from the insurance company—but at that point it was a bit like getting permission to give someone a parachute after they've been pushed out of the plane and grew wings on their own (to paraphrase Ray Bradbury).

I went on to do another twenty issues of *StarChild,* which we reprinted and sold in hardcover and paperback collections, as well as in hundred-dollar limited collector's editions. All told, we eventually sold nearly a quarter of a million copies of comic books that should never have existed, except for a single choice—to decide that I was *right*.

That single choice formed the basis of my entire career, because I had made that choice when everyone else in the world—even people who loved me and cared about me—told me it was not possible. I held firmly onto what I believed was most true. And with the help of people who believed in me, and supported me, and helped me, I made it happen.

Nothing—*nothing*—you really want to make happen is over until you decide to stop. And if you really want to make it happen, no reason, no excuse, will ever be big enough to make you stop.

Pessimism leads to weakness.

Optimism leads to power.

WILLIAM JAMES

PART III

Never, ever, sacrifice what
you want the most,
for what you want the most
at that moment.

*The man who has no more problems
to solve, is out of the game.*

<small>ELBERT HUBBARD</small>

CHAPTER SEVEN

MOTION DOES NOT ALWAYS EQUAL PROGRESS

I f you can produce, you can survive; if you can produce consistently, you can thrive. And every so often, the floodgates open, and you are presented with more opportunities than you believed possible.

The success of *StarChild* led to other projects in different creative fields, and I started getting involved in publishing magazines. I reinvigorated a hundred-year-old arts magazine called *International Studio* and prepared to leverage my name recognition with the comics and genre bookstores to relaunch it as a high-end arts periodical. I also began writing and publishing collections of short stories (which was mostly an excuse to design the books), and I started working on a couple of novels. But unlike earlier in my career, I never stopped working on new comic books. I'd never leave that behind again—not completely.

I was doing the work that I believed I was supposed to be doing. I was doing the creative work that I believed was my destiny, but I still had another lesson to learn. I was still missing something that was somehow necessary to my becoming who I was meant to be. And that lesson came about in part because of the magazines.

I had been getting some fan mail from a comics fan in Germany who basically loved my books. He loved *StarChild,* and he sent me some very nice letters—the kind that are too glowing to really believe, but too ego-boosting not to keep.

In preparing the first test issue of *International Studio,* we had a French writer serving as our European Correspondent who had to drop out at the last minute, leaving a hole in the magazine we could fill, and a hole in the masthead that we couldn't.

We believed that a magazine with the word "International" in the title really needed a European Correspondent, and we racked our brains to figure out whom we might get to fill the position. Then my brother casually mentioned the German comics fan. He was European, and since I'd written him back, we were technically corresponding. That worked for me, so we stuck his name in the magazine and sent it to the printer.

The issue—which had bound-in art prints and tipped-in sketchbooks, and was basically a very expensive marvel of production—was beautiful, sold well, and was priced way too low. But it was a good dry run, and we learned a lot from doing it. Not long after it was released, I got a fax from the German comics fan.

He said he'd just gotten the new magazine, which he really liked, and he'd noticed that he was listed on the masthead as our European Correspondent, which was why he was writing the letter.

He said that he'd really rather we'd asked him about it first, but that if having his name in the magazine would improve our relationship with the European publishing community, then it was fine to leave it in.

I sent him a profuse apology in response, then asked him, respectfully, why adding the name of a comics fan would enhance the magazine's reputation in Europe.

He answered with a suggestion I ought to look him up online. So I did.

It turned out that this fellow, Kai Meyer, my comics fan, the guy who adored *StarChild,* was basically the Stephen King of Germany. He's one of the most popular authors in Europe, having written dozens of novels, and a double-handful of top-of-the-sales-charts best-selling novels. His children's books outsell the Harry Potter series in Asia. He's had several movies made from his work. As authors go, he basically has a huge footprint—and I had just stuck his name in my magazine.

After that, Kai became one of my best friends, and we started a correspondence and a friendship that has lasted to this day.

Somewhere along the way, he asked me if I'd ever thought about writing a prose novel. Not more comic books like *StarChild*, but a straight words-only prose novel. I said I'd thought about it, and I had even written a very bad novel (as all novelists must when they're starting out, and which, in a prescient bit of foreshadowing, I called *The Barbizon Diaries*), and asked him why he wanted to know.

Kai said he'd gotten a little too expensive for his previous publishers, but that they still wanted to find a way to work with him. They proposed that he create and edit a series of novels called MythWorld. Kai would supply the initial premise for the series, lend his name to it for marketing purposes, and personally edit the novels, which would be written by other, less-well-known authors.

Kai said he'd written a three-page outline for a seven-book series, and he thought maybe I'd like to write one of the books—perhaps the second or third. I thought that was a stellar idea and asked him to send over the outline.

The central premise was easy enough to grasp: somehow, a performance of Wagner's *Ring Cycle* operas creates an event that de-evolves the entire world into a pre-industrial, mythological state. But my part—about a Russian journalist who turns into the witch Baba Yaga—was all of *two paragraphs long*. Somehow, I was supposed to get a two-hundred page novel out of that.

I'd never really written a prose book before—except for the bad one—so I sat down and plowed through it as if it were just one of my comic books, but without the pictures. I threw everything I had into it and put in all the fun stuff I like in novels: mythology, and droll humor, and ancient books, and magic, and talking dogs, and even a little sexy stuff. The only really hard part was that I was writing a second novel with no clue what the author of the first book in the series was going to do.

I turned it in with the caveat that I knew they'd probably have to change some things about the characters and situations that didn't even exist in the first book yet.

Kai responded by saying it wouldn't be a problem

because none of the other six authors, including the writer expected to write book one, had written a *single word* yet.

I went out and bought a case of Diet Dr. Pepper and locked myself in the studio for a weekend. I came out on Monday with twenty pages of notes for six more MythWorld books, including a book one that meshed perfectly with my book two.

Kai and the publisher were duly impressed with both the effort I'd put forth and the story I'd crafted. And since at that point, I'd done more work on the books than anyone else, including Kai, they gave the assignment to write the rest of the books, as well as ownership of the entire series, to me.

In Germany, it's still titled *Kai Meyer's MythWorld,* written by James Owen, but in the rest of the world it's entirely mine. The first book, *Festival of Bones,* won the AI Award for Best International Novel, and was shortlisted for several others. (Stephen King beat me out on one award, but I got more votes than Michael Crichton, so that's okay.)

Four of the originally planned seven books came out in hardcover in Germany, and two in paperback, before I parted ways with the publisher over issues of payment and the direction of the series. Ultimately Mythworld grew to a planned series of fifteen books, five of which I wrote.

The first two books were published in France by Studio Malens, who also published the French edition of the first *StarChild* book. As of this writing, parts of a prequel graphic novel called *Obscuro* were published by Image Comics, but only the first two MythWorld novels themselves have been published in English. That may change however. All good things happen . . . In Time.

Writing several novels back-to-back gave me an incredible education in a hurry, and I gained the experience I'd need for when it was time to sit down and write the Imaginarium Geographica novels. Because I'd written and illustrated six hundred pages of *StarChild* material, I had the confidence and skill to illustrate them, too.

The Imaginarium Geographica novels were still in my future, but I had learned something about myself, something that had worried me since my car accident. Thanks to Kai, I was now a *novelist*. I could create something of quality, even without pictures. That gave me confidence, which is a useful trait to have, especially since you never know when a disaster is about to happen.

After having lived in Washington for several years, my family returned to Arizona where I began working at an animation studio in Phoenix as Director of Creative Services. Ironically, I was working with and supervising artists whom I would have worked under had we all stayed with their original employer: the Sullivan Bluth Studio in Ireland.

The comics market had undergone a downturn, and my German publisher was splitting into two companies, which was delaying publication of the MythWorld books. My detour back into animation was mostly to put bread on the table. To outward appearances, there was a lot going on in my career. But motion does not always equal progress. Twenty miles on an exercycle is good for my health, but not good for getting somewhere else. And most of the work I did during this time was pedaling on an exercycle.

The one ambition I hoped would change all of that was a bolder foray into magazine publishing. I had added the classic pulp magazine *Argosy* to *International Studio,* and I was mulling over plans to launch an entire line of magazines. *Argosy* was the venue where Tarzan first appeared, and many classic writers had graced its pages. With these magazines, I envisioned a return to those glory days, in both art and literature.

The best way to summarize the entire venture into

magazines is to say that it was a grand experiment that won many design awards, scored excellent reviews, and lost a great deal of money.

Both periodicals were high class, high quality publications. *International Studio* was oversized, in beautiful full color, and was priced more appropriately than its predecessor. *Argosy* was actually produced as two square-bound volumes in a slipcase—very high end for a magazine. We had some distinguished advertisers—some of whom I'd courted since the first issue of *International Studio,* in the late 1990s—who were willing to back us if we could meet our sales and circulation goals. Everything seemed perfect, and both magazines were extremely well-received by everyone who saw them, which was a far, far smaller number than we'd hoped for.

The arts magazine sold well, but our distributor *completely* crashed with *Argosy*. There were problems with the format, which they didn't like, and delays in dealing with those problems completely wrecked the schedule. The winter issue did not go out until spring, which did not make the advertisers happy. I promised to correct the problems with the follow-up issue, which was even more beautiful than the first—and which ended up sitting in a warehouse.

At that point, we realized the distributor was having problems of their own, but by then, it was already too late. We published a special Bob Peak issue of *International Studio* to accompany a gallery show in New York, and a third issue of *Argosy,* mostly to fulfill subscriptions and because we'd already paid for all the material, and for all intents and purposes, that was it for us, as far as mainstream magazine publication was concerned.

Several other publishers working with the same distributor had gone through similar problems, and we spent a lot of time and money arguing back and forth about how badly they had messed everything up without getting them to take responsibility or make good on our lost revenues. But that was a secondary problem. The primary problem was that I had financed everything *myself*. All the editorial costs, author payments, and production and publishing costs were on my shoulders. And with only a few distribution mistakes, all the revenue that was supposed to have paid those costs *vanished*.

An editor I'm friends with got in touch and pointed out that several other magazine publishers who were a lot better funded than I was had gone down in flames over similar circumstances. Furthermore, he predicted that my efforts to get the distributor to pony up the money for the

mishandled and missing magazines would come to nothing
and that I'd never see another penny from them. I agreed
with him on all counts.

"You have a lot of debts," he told me. "A *huge* amount
of debt. You're going to be in a lot of trouble. What are you
going to do?"

I said I'd considered all my options, and I really
had only one viable choice open to me that would fix
everything.

"What I've got to do," I told him, "is write and sell a
best-selling novel. And then I have to get a movie deal
for a gazillion dollars. And when I've done both of those
things, everything's going to be just *fine*. So I appreciate
your concern, but don't worry—I've *got* this."

His only reply was "God be with you, James."

But I believed it was possible to do exactly what I said
I'd do, so I loaded up my books, and my outlines, and my
notes, and my comics, and everything else creative I could
fit in my van, and I headed for Los Angeles for meetings
with my managers and my agent to see what I could sell.

Motion can simply be made to happen. Progress has
to be *earned*.

Genius is only the power of making continuous efforts. The line between failure and success is so fine that we scarcely know when we pass it: so fine that we are often on the line and do not know it. How many a man has thrown up his hands at a time when a little more effort, a little more patience, would have achieved success.

ELBERT HUBBARD

CHAPTER EIGHT

VALUE WHAT YOU DO, AND OTHERS WILL, TOO

Doing quality work, consistently, opens up more opportunities to do good work, but as I've written in my novels, "All good things happen . . . In Time." Choices are cumulative, but the results are not always apparent, or immediate. Sometimes you just have to keep making the right choices, even if it seems there's no benefit to doing so. Sooner or later, there will come a moment when what you really want most is tested, and how you respond in that moment will reveal the culmination of your choices.

On that first ambitious trip to Los Angeles, I was there for nine weeks and could hardly get a meeting with anyone, much less sell anything. When I finally started getting meetings, nobody bought anything. I was at a point where everything in the world was about to crash down on me.

I had just enough money left for either gas or food, and I was saving the money for gas in case I had one more meeting. I hadn't eaten anything in about four days, and I was too embarrassed to tell the friends I was staying with (after my motel money ran out) just how broke I was.

My house was in foreclosure. My Studio was in foreclosure. The utilities were being turned off. I hadn't been able to pay my employees. I was being sued by printers and others to whom I owed money on the magazines. And I basically had just a few dollars left, which I refused to use for food because a dollar's worth of gas could get me to Sony, and three dollars could get me to Disney, and a buck sixty-five could get me to Paramount. And I just needed *one more meeting*, where I knew I could sell *something*.

Suddenly, in the middle of all this, I got a phone call from a publisher who wanted to talk about my novels.

He'd called the Studio, where Jeremy (my brother and Studio manager) told him that I'd love to talk to him and could return his call once I found the gas money to drive home. The publisher asked if I had a cell phone—I did; a Virgin Mobile phone with about sixteen dollars left on it—and Jeremy gave him the number.

The publisher, whom I'd known casually for a number of years, pointed out that the MythWorld books hadn't been published in English yet and said he'd like to be the one to do it. But he'd also heard about this outline I had floating around—something about Dragons, and a mysterious atlas of maps to imaginary lands—and suggested that we start with that, then see if we could also do something with MythWorld. I thought that all sounded fantastic.

Then he topped his own offer. He said he'd talked with my Studio manager, and he knew we were in a tight spot.

"James, I think you're a good guy," he said to me, "so I'll tell you what—if you'll basically give me a gentleman's agreement over the phone, right now, to do this *Here, There Be Dragons* book, I will wire you the book advance tomorrow."

That *never* happens in publishing. It usually takes months to get a contract, and more months after that to get the book advance. Even so, the average book advance for a hardcover is about ten thousand dollars, and I needed a whole lot more than that. But no one else was offering me anything, so I asked as casually as I could just how much he was offering.

"Five thousand dollars," he said. "Just say yes, and you'll have the money tomorrow."

That put me in a difficult spot. *Dragons* was something I was actively shopping as a movie, with a much bigger payday in mind. But he had said he wanted to discuss MythWorld too, so a larger offer might be forthcoming. The key was he was willing to send the money right away. And no one else was offering me anything.

I thought about it, and I decided I'd be crazy to say no. I needed to say yes, because while the advance wouldn't come close to resolving all my debts, it would let me pay some bills. I could pay the mortgage. I could pay my utilities and my employees. I could get gas money and go home for a few days. I could get a hamburger. (The hamburger may have been the highest priority.) But the money could keep me going, and I told myself I could come back and get the deal I needed to get, and make up the difference on the film deal. And so I told him yes.

I borrowed some money from my friends to start driving home, and the publisher went to make the arrangements for the wire. An hour later he called me and said, "James, I'm so excited! I've always wanted to work with you. This is great. It's going to be a beautiful paperback book."

I nearly wrecked the car.

I gathered my wits and, as calmly as I could, I explained that *Here, There Be Dragons* had to be released in hardcover.

What I was thinking about was the Stephen King story about his first book, *Carrie*. He sold it in hardcover for a few thousand dollars—but he sold the paperback rights for *four hundred thousand dollars*. That's what launched his career. I'd done the same thing (on a smaller scale) with the first two MythWorld novels, where the paperback advances were fifteen times what I'd been paid for the hardcovers.

But you can't go backwards—you can't start with a paperback and then go to a hardcover. That pretty much never happens unless you're Stephen King or maybe Garth Nix.

The publisher said he'd done all the numbers and just didn't think he could sell more than five thousand copies, which is still a pretty respectable number, especially for a new author, which is what I'd be. He insisted he couldn't afford to do it as a hardcover, but said if I'd still say yes, he'd give me another thousand dollars on the advance.

My response was to say that if he'd just do the book in hardcover, I'd take a thousand *less*.

We argued that way all the way to Blythe, which is a terrible place to be discussing your entire future while you're at a point that you would almost justify running over a bunch of Girl Scouts selling puppies in exchange for a hamburger.

He and I argued on my cell phone for three hours, until I was nearly out of minutes. We ended up at an impasse. I was willing to take so little money it would barely be considered a professional sale. He had raised his offer high enough that we were almost at the average advance for a hardcover book. And neither one of us was willing to budge.

Finally, I made the hardest decision I've ever made in my life, and I told him no.

I hung up the phone, and spent the next six hours driving home. I redialed his number probably a thousand times, thinking of every reason why I should say yes, before hanging up again. I'd already told my family and friends I was coming home and that we were getting money. I said we'd be able to pay some bills and hold off a few creditors. And I was starving.

But I held out and never actually called him back.

When I got home, I gathered everyone together—friends, family, employees, a few creditors—and told them what had happened, including the fact I'd just turned down almost twice the amount I said we'd be getting.

And then I said that they needed to trust me, because it was the right decision, and somehow, I would work everything out.

"You've trusted me so far, trust me now," I told them. "This was the right choice. Trust me."

They all said that they would.

Right about then, a friend of mine showed up at the door. He'd heard I'd gotten a book deal and had come over to celebrate.

I told him to come in, but that he'd better sit down. We explained to him what had happened, and he listened to the whole thing without saying a word. When we'd finished, he looked at me and asked, "Was it the right choice?"

I said it was *absolutely* the right choice.

"Well, then," he said, "you need to get your rear back to Los Angeles and go get the right deal."

I said that was indeed my plan, and as soon as we could figure out how to actually keep everything turned on and stapled together so I could afford to go back, I would.

He looked at me and asked how much money I'd turned down. I told him the number. He pulled out his checkbook, and he wrote me a check for that exact amount and handed it to me.

"You're making the right choices," he said as he got up to leave, "and you always have. Now you go do what you need to do, because your friends have got your back. We believe in you, and we're not going to let you fall."

And he left. As I stood there holding the check, I realized I was looking at the culmination of my choices.

His father was the banker who had given me my first business loan when I was sixteen years old.

Now, almost two decades later, his son realized I was still following the path I'd chosen long ago, and that I just needed some help along the way.

If you make that hard choice to do what you believe in most, people find ways to help you.

The decision I made on that drive from Los Angeles involved a choice. The most important choice I make about everything on a daily basis. The most important lesson I teach in person or in my books. The one lesson I hope you remember.

Never, ever sacrifice what you want the *most,* for what you want the most *at that moment.*

What I had wanted most at that moment was a hamburger.

What I wanted the most was the right publishing deal. And I held out.

I went back to Los Angeles, and it took another couple of months of meetings and people not doing anything, not buying anything, before finally . . . *finally*, I had That Meeting.

I had that meeting with someone who said, "I think my boss will like what you do." And his boss was the producer of the Harry Potter films. Then some months later, my manager called and said we'd gotten a pre-emptive offer (which means really high) from Simon & Schuster, who wanted to publish *Here, There Be Dragons*—in hardcover.

The week the book was published, Warner Brothers optioned the rights for just under a gazillion dollars. The book is now in its *eighth* hardcover printing, its *tenth* paper-back printing, and is being published in more than twenty-two languages. Hundreds of thousands of copies have been sold; six sequels are following it, and the movie is being worked on by the producers of *Lord of the Rings*.

A choice with no consequences has no value. Making a choice knowing there will be consequences, and be-ing willing to bear them, is what distinguishes the right choices from the wrong ones.

I learned . . . that if one advances confidently in the direction of his dreams, and endeavors to live the life he has imagined, he will meet with success unexpected in common hours.

Henry David Thoreau

CHAPTER NINE

TO BE HAPPY, AND TO
HELP OTHER PEOPLE

Most of the really interesting questions I get at my live presentations come from the kids. Usually it's things like "Do you know J.K. Rowling?" (No), or, "Do you know Stephenie Meyer?" (Yes), or "Are you rich?" (I can order pizza whenever I want), or questions about whether my dog missed me when I went to Ireland (Definitely, yes).

A lot of them ask to see my Superman ring, and sometimes they ask to look at my right hand, which feels fine but still looks a bit crooked. But every once in a while, a kid asks me a question that just flattens me.

A few years ago, I spoke at a school for homeless kids in San Diego. The students literally have no homes. They would come to school, do their work, and leave, going . . .

somewhere. After my presentation, one of the students, a mild, petite girl, raised her hand to ask me a question.

"Mr. Owen," she said when I called on her, "do you ever wonder what would have happened if you had actually called that publisher back and told him yes?"

"Sweetheart," I said, "I wonder that every day. It's one of the things I think about when I'm trying to make other choices."

"So," she said, "you didn't know it would work out, but you just believed it would."

"Yes."

"Good," she said with a look of relief, "because I didn't know if things would work out for me and my family, but now I think I believe they can."

Then she gave me a hug and left, smiling.

My heart just broke with love for the simple, pure faith of that little girl who was willing to change how she looked at her world because someone she believed, someone she trusted, said that they believed in her, too. And perhaps for the first time, I realized that not everyone had someone like my grandfather, who could tell me with absolute sincerity that he believed in me and would always be there for me.

Not everyone was raised with the spiritual beliefs

I was taught, which helped me in finding my purpose; I always believed there was a Creator who had given me the gifts and the guidance I needed to fulfill that purpose. Not everyone had someone in their lives who believed in magic. So I resolved to become that person for as many people as possible, to tell them they had a greater destiny than they believed, and that I had faith that they could fulfill it.

I say these things to people young and old, and people see in my face and hear in my voice that I believe in them, and in that moment, they have the chance to change anything and everything about their lives.

How much greater could those moments be if there were more voices added to my own?

Sometimes people ask how it was possible to get through as many trials as I've had, and overcome the obstacles I've faced. I tell them it's a bit like imagining your life as a book.

In any good book, there are always going to be sections of strife and grief for the characters. It might last for a few pages, or it might be a whole chapter, or more. The important thing to remember is that the story always continues. The grief only lasts as long as it takes to read those pages, then it's over, and the story takes a better course.

If you think of your life as a story, then you can think of any grief or stress you might be experiencing as just a few pages—and *anyone* can get through a few pages. You are the author of your own story, the illustrator of your own destiny. You choose the words and the lines that fill its pages.

The important thing to remember about choices is that it's always possible to make them. No matter what's happening in your life, you can decide how to respond— and you can choose what to do next. Always.

Even if you've made a string of bad choices—which I'll be first to admit having done, far more often than I'd have liked—you can still redeem those bad choices in how you choose to accept the consequences they caused to happen.

Admitting your faults isn't a weakness; it's a *strength*. Having your weaknesses pointed out isn't a slur on your character; it's an opportunity to improve your life.

I wanted to share this message when I realized that while the students I spoke to were interested in the books, they were more interested in knowing how I was able to do this for a living. The answer to that question goes far beyond "Finish your novel before you query an agent," or advice about good grammar and punctuation. I realized that what they wanted to hear was something far, far more fundamental. A truth that's ever more clearly essential to kids like that little girl in San Diego.

My first real mentor was a man named Larry Austin. He was an English teacher, the local Presbyterian minister, and a philosopher. When I was a kid, he'd loan me books out of his overflowing garage library which I'd read and return a week or two later. Then we'd sit and discuss the books while playing chess, drinking Vernors' Ginger Ale, and listening to Barry Manilow albums. He never talked down to me, and more often than not beat me soundly in our chess games. But I learned a lot from him, including his distillation of what he believed were the key points of all human philosophy.

To Larry, all questions could be boiled down into just two: Am I important? And can I survive?

On a trip to visit him in Michigan, I told him I'd managed to distill my own life philosophy into just two goals, under which everything else was covered: to be happy, and to help other people.

I've been working hard at living up to both of those goals ever since.

At times, people who focus on the positive instead of the negative seem to have charmed lives. As my friend, the actor and art-lover Peter MacNicol put it, I seemed to have had "an endless run of green lights." But that was before he heard the story about the car accident.

Still, it's always better to focus on what's going right instead of what's gone wrong. Someone once said that entrepreneurs can fail a hundred times, but all that is washed away with one smashing win. That is why I advocate determination as such a strong and necessary trait, because when people see you are determined to do something, they feel inspired to try to help you.

It's basically the old children's story *Stone Soup,* where a fellow goes into town and asks for food, but no one will give him anything. So he borrows a kettle, fills it with water, starts a fire, and plunks a stone into the water.

After a while, someone gets curious and asks what he's doing. He tells them he's making stone soup, which he'll be happy to share, as soon as it's ready. The passerby sits down, having never tasted soup made from a stone. "It's almost ready," the man says, sipping at the soup, "but it's too bad I have no carrots, for that would make it perfect."

"I have some carrots!" the villager says, and he rushes to get them. In the meantime, someone else asks about the soup, and the man says, "I'm happy to share it with you. I'm only sorry that I have no potatoes, because then you'd really love it."

In time, all the villagers who had turned the traveler away come by to look at the miraculous stone soup, and all of them bring a little something to "make it just *perfect.*" And when it was all done, they all marveled at how he made such delicious soup from nothing but a stone.

Someone who has nothing and complains about their fate only drives people away. But someone who insists he can make something wonderful out of what seems to be the most impossible of ingredients draws to himself the power of the Universe. And people see that in his face; they hear it in his voice. And they find ways to help him.

Confidence is often mistaken for arrogance, and I've had my share of critics who think that when I'm talking about quality in my work, I'm boasting. I'm not. As the old saying goes, "It ain't bragging if you done it." But more to the point, I don't think there's anything wrong with being proud of doing something well. In fact, if you intend to do something creative for a living, it's absolutely *essential.*

Proper pride is the feeling you experience when you know you have done something well—and there's nothing wrong with expressing that. Proper pride is when you say "I am good at what I do"; improper pride is when you say

"I can do this better than you can." There's nothing wrong with being good at what you do, and knowing that you are, but there is no value in belittling the work of someone else while praising your own.

We are all running our own race, and no one should be out to do anything but finish with your head held high, knowing that you ran the best race you were able to.

False humility is also something to be avoided. Real humility is gratitude—gratitude for being able to use the gifts you have to enrich your life and the lives of those around you. False humility is merely fear—fear that someone might take offense to your confidence and to your belief in the quality of your work. And it's impossible to make anything extraordinary happen if you are constantly belittling your own work.

Several years ago, while I was developing *International Studio,* I had the opportunity to meet with the CEO of a large media company. We were discussing a possible investment in my magazine, and I'd sent him a framed print of the cover art as a calling card. He thought my approach was intriguing enough that he asked to meet.

When I arrived, we spoke for over an hour, discussing magazines, and my career, and my hopes for the future. Then he paused, looked at me, and asked, "What *are* you?"

I blinked, and asked what he meant.

He clarified by asking, if I was to describe myself, how would I do it? Was I a writer, or an artist, or an entrepreneur? Was I a scholar or a publisher? What was I?

I asked if he was asking what I did, or what I was. He understood the distinction and chose the latter. I thought a moment, drew in a breath, and answered, "Sir, I am a Merchant Prince, in training to become a Philosopher King." He didn't ask me what I meant by that. He already knew.

His company never did invest in my magazines, but that was okay. I learned a lot from that meeting, as I have from every other experience I've ever had, good and bad. Every moment is another chance to learn, and another chance to make a choice.

Everything does happen for a reason, and the things that happened were supposed to happen, because they *did* happen. And while no one can change the past, the future begins anew every time you choose to live deliberately.

Those who make miracles happen are the ones who, first, believe it to be possible, and second, are willing to pay the price to make it so.

Some people see what I chose to do as "enduring," but I think the idea of simply "enduring to the end" is a terrible philosophy and an awful way to live one's life. How you spend your days is how you live your life, and if you're spending them "enduring" anything then you're doing it wrong. I feel the same way about regret. If everything in the past has value, then there's no reason for regret, ever.

With no regret and no fear, there's nothing left but possibility, and joy. And the realization that it is a wonderful world we live in, after all.

We are the music-makers,
And we are the dreamers of dreams,
Wandering by lone sea-breakers,
And sitting by desolate streams;
World-losers and world-forsakers,
On whom the pale moon gleams:
Yet we are the movers and shakers
Of the world for ever, it seems.

ARTHUR O'SHAUGHNESSY

*On that hill, silently and solemnly,
Superboy promised himself and who or
whatever else might hear his thoughts
that he would use his powers whenever
possible to save and improve the
conditions of life and of living things
everywhere; that under no circumstances
would he ever be responsible for the loss
of a single conscious life; that failing
in any of these affirmations he would
renounce his powers forever. There
could be no nobler mission
for a superman.*

ELLIOT S! MAGGIN

EPILOGUE

DRAWING OUT
THE DRAGONS

Dragons have long been presented in legends and fables as terrifying creatures, which they certainly can be. Even in my own heritage, the Millett family crest, they are an example of a tyrannical creature to be defeated.

I think the things that make us feel fear in this life are very much like Dragons.

While they're up in the cave at the edge of the village—hidden, mysterious, unknown—we build up in our heads the image of what we think might be up there, but without ever really knowing the truth.

Only by approaching the Dragon and drawing it out can we discover that not only is there no reason to fear, but also that confronting the Dragon changes the way we see the world.

You may have heard the saying, "Do the thing you fear, and the death of fear is certain." That is absolutely true.

In my Imaginarium Geographica books, the phrase "Here, there be Dragons" recurs over and over again. On the mariner's map in our world (from which the phrase was taken), it was meant as a warning. But in my stories, it's meant as a comfort.

Dragons are the guardians of the Earth and of the creatures who live in it. "Here, there be Dragons" means that something bigger, older, stronger, and perhaps wiser, is looking out for you.

So draw out your Dragons; confront your fears; and remember—as long as you have the power to choose, there will always be a way to change the course of events in your life.

The last thing I usually do during one of my presentations is a drawing demonstration. I began to do it after I started telling the story about the car accident and my right hand. People would look at the cover illustration of *Here, There Be Dragons* (which is similar to the cover illustration of this book), and they usually comment on the fact that there seem to be a million tiny lines in the drawing—lines it would be impossible for anyone else to make.

I gently remind them that I have shared with them the Secret of Drawing—making lines on paper, and choosing where they go—and that once you know how to begin with the very first lines, anyone can draw a Dragon. Anyone. Because all it takes to start . . .

. . . is just *four lines.*

And everyone can draw four lines. Everyone. All you need is for someone who's drawn them before to show you where they begin. So I do—on stage, with a big, fat marker, so everyone can see.

I start with four lines, then four more, then one or two more—at which point there's usually an audible gasp from the audience, because already, the Dragon has started to take shape.

I continue to add details, and, as I draw, I explain that making choices in the drawing of a Dragon is just like the choices we make in living our lives. It's cumulative.

Every line is a choice. Every decision you make in your life is a choice. I keep drawing as I remind them about the stories I've shared, and the events which seemed catastrophic at the time, but which set the groundwork for everything wonderful that was to come after.

Sometimes that meant seeing something that no one else could see. At times in your life you may have to tell people "I'm going to draw a Dragon," and when you start with those first four lines, they just don't see it. They may not understand; they might tell you what you're doing is impossible, but *that's* when it's most important for you to believe in yourself and in what you've chosen to do.

Keep adding lines, and keep making choices, because sooner or later, you'll have added enough lines. Sooner or later, you'll have made enough of the right choices that you can step back . . .

. . . and everyone can see you were drawing a Dragon all along.

A Dragon that began with four simple lines that anyone can draw, if someone shows them how.

It's very much the same with choices—and the reason I wrote this book.

There was an anecdote on an episode of *The West Wing* television series about someone who had fallen into a deep hole. He shouted for help, and finally, someone heard him. But instead of throwing him a rope or something similar, the second guy jumps down into the hole with him.

"Why did you do that?" the first guy says. "Now we're both stuck down here."

"I jumped down here with you," the second guy answers, "because I've been down here before—and I know how to get out."

These examples, these stories I've been sharing with you, are the first few lines you need to draw out your own Dragons—not to battle with them, but to embrace them, to make their strength your own, and to perhaps, one day, become like them: a wiser, stronger protector and teacher, with stories of your own you can use to inspire and elevate those around you.

Choices are inevitable—there's no way to avoid them. So—take a deep breath. Choose the line you want to make. And draw.

What you create from there is *entirely* up to you. But remember: *I believe in you. And I will not let you fall.*

HERE, THERE BE DRAGONS

How to draw a Dragon ~ by James A. Owen

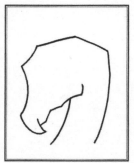

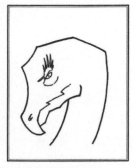

STEP 1: Start at the top and draw downwards, making the outline of the Dragon's head and beak.

STEP 2: Draw the top of his head, then the back of his head, then the back of his neck. Add his lower jaw and the front of his neck.

STEP 3: Add the top of his jaw, a nostril in his beak, and his eye and eyebrow. And don't worry—he just looks mean!

STEP 4: Add the fins that run down his back. This is important—Dragons are very particular about their fins.

STEP 5: Add the large plate scales, beginning across from his eye and going down his neck. Then add a forehead ridge.

STEP 6: Now you get to add the details that give him his character—shadowing, spines, feathers, and fur. And there's your Dragon!

AFTERWORD

I. If you really want to do something, no one can stop you, but if you really don't want to do something, no one can help you.

II. Live deliberately. Decide: Are you the kind of person things happen to, or the kind of person who makes things happen?

III. Never, ever, sacrifice what you want the most, for what you want the most at that moment.

Also recall the Secret of Drawing, which consists of just two things: One, making lines on paper; and two, choosing where they go.

Every drawing, every life, is nothing but a series of choices and actions. The lines I made as a child are the same as those I make as an adult, because it's the same mind making the choices. Make your lines. Make your choices. It's always entirely in your hands.

And finally, my last lesson. When I draw a Dragon at a presentation, inevitably someone asks if they can have it. And I bring them onstage . . . and *give* it to them.

Always, *always* ask for what you want. Because the Universe might surprise you—and give it to you.

Magic is real. And worth looking for.

BIBLIOGRAPHY

Allen, James. *As a Man Thinketh*. Salt Lake City: Deseret Book, 2002.

Bryan, William Jennings. *Speeches of William Jennings Bryan, Volume 2*. New York: Funk & Wagnalls, 1913.

Frost, Robert. "Two Tramps in Mud Time." *The Poetry of Robert Frost: The Collected Poems, Complete and Unabridged*. Edited by Edward Connery Latham. New York: Henry Holt, 1969.

Goethe, Johann Wolfgang von. *Faust*. Translated by John Anster. N.p.: London, 1835.

Hammarskjold, Dag. *Markings*. Canada: Knopf, 1964.

Hubbard, Elbert. *The Note Book of Elbert Hubbard*. N.p.: The Roycrofters, 1927.

James, William. *The Varieties of Religious Experience*. New York: Random House, 1902.

Maggin, Elliot S! *Superman: Last Son of Krypton*. New York: Warner Books, 1978.

Martin, Steve. "An hour with Steve Martin." Interview by Charlie Rose. *Charlie Rose*. December 12, 2007. http://www.charlierose.com/view/interview/8831.

O'Shaughnessy, Arthur. *Music and Moonlight: Poems and Songs*. London: Chatto and Windus Publishers, 1874.

Thoreau, Henry David. *Walden: An Annotated Edition*. Edited by Walter Harding. New York: Houghton Mifflin, 1949.

Twain, Mark. In Wayne Ashmore and Jennifer Nualt. *My Favorite Writer: Mark Twain*. New York: Weigl, 2009.

Van Gogh, Vincent. In Steven Naifeh and Gregory White Smith. *Van Gogh: The Life*. New York: Random House, 2011.

Ziglar, Zig. *See You at the Top: 25th Anniversary Edition*. Gretna: Pelican, 2005.

THE MEDITATIONS

Author JAMES A. OWEN shares his personal story
in this profound trilogy of insight and inspiration.
Filled with memorable stories and deep truths, these books
will challenge you and change you and increase
your desire to live an extraordinary life.

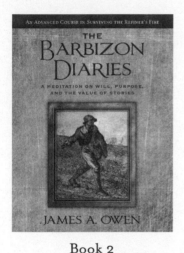

Book 2	Book 3
SUMMER 2013	**FALL 2013**
978-1-60907-393-0	978-1-60907-418-0
$19.99	$19.99